51 Dump Cake Recipes

Scrumptious Dump Cake Desserts To Satisfy Your Sweet Tooth

By Brianne Heaton

© Revelry Publishing 2014

Scrumptious Desserts To Satisfy Your Sweet Tooth

Copyright 2014 by Revelry Publishing

All Rights reserved under International and Pan-American Copyright Conventions. By payment of required fees, you have been granted the non-exclusive, non-transferable right to access and read the text of this book. No part of this text may be reproduced, transmitted, downloaded, decompiled, reverse-engineered or stored in or introduced into any information storage and retrieval system, in any form or by any means, whether electronic or mechanical, now known, hereinafter invented, without express written permission of the publisher.

DISCLAIMER

All information in this book has been carefully researched and checked for factual accuracy. However, the authors and publishers make no warranty, express or implied, that the information contained herein is appropriate for every individual, situation or purpose, and assume no responsibility for errors or omissions. The reader assumes the risk and full responsibility for all actions, and the authors will not be held responsible for any loss or damage, whether consequential, incidental, special or otherwise that may result from the information presented in this publication.

We have relied on our own experience as well as many different sources for this book, and we have done our best to check facts and to give credit where it is due. In the event that any material is incorrect or has been used without proper permission, please contact us so that the oversight can be corrected.

ISBN-13: 978-0993941542
ISBN-10: 0993941540

Other books by Brianne Heaton:

56 Breakfast Sandwich Recipes: Irresistible Sandwich Ideas to Kickstart Your Morning

Breakfast is the most important meal of the day so it makes sense to treat it so. Are you finding it difficult to get the right balance and variety of taste experiences every day? With breakfast sandwich mania in full swing, there is no shortage of breakfast ideas here.

50 Holiday Dessert Recipes: Delectable Dessert Ideas For The Christmas Holidays And Other Special Occasions

Wow your family and friends with the most decadent cakes, creamiest cheesecakes, most delicious cookies, juiciest pies and most interesting international desserts! It's time to bring the baker in you to the surface and make the best desserts ever! Indulge in these holiday delights with the confidence of having made it yourself!

51 Easter Dessert Ideas: Scrumptious Easter Recipes For Any Occasion

This holiday cookbook collection of 51 Easter dessert recipes has something tasty and enticing for everyone, and you don't have to be Julia Child in order to pull them off. The recipes can also be used for other special occasions.

46 Sriracha Flavored Recipes: Delicious Sriracha Hot Sauce Cookbook For A Spicy Palate

Check out these delectable dessert, appetizer, entree, and drink recipes and see how Sriracha can enrich even the dullest of meals. Follow our meal plan for a whole week full of delicious Sriracha meals. Your taste buds will thank you for it.

Get the latest update on new releases from the author at:

https://www.brianneheaton.com/newsletter

Table of Contents

Introduction 1
Apple 3
   1 - Apple Pie Dump Cake 5
   2 - Blueberry Apple Dump Cake 7
   3 - Golden Dump Cake 8
   4 - Spiced Apple Pecan Dump Cake 9
   5 - Homemade French Apple Dump Cake 10
   6 - Cinnamon Apple Dump Cake 12
Berries 13
   7 - Everything Berry Dump Cake 15
   8 - Double Blackberry Dump Cake 17
   9 - Blueberry Lemon Dump Cake 18
   10 - Crumbly Blackberry Dump Cake 19
   11 - Raspberry Vanilla Dump Cake 21
   12 - Crunchy Blueberry Dump Cake 22
   13 - Fresh Blueberry Dump Cake 23
Cherry 25
   14 - Cherry Angel Dump Cake 27
   15 - Cherry Crock Pot Dump Cake 28
   16 - Cherry Pineapple Dump Cake 29
   17 - Nutty Cherry Dump Cake 31
   18 - Dark Cherry Black Forest Dump Cake 32
   19 - Cherry Choco Cola Dump Cake 33
Citrus 35
   20 - Mandarin Dump Cake 37
   21 - Lemon Delight Dump Cake 38
   22 - Chocolate Orange Surprise Dump Cake 39
Peach 40
   23 - Southern Style Peach Dump Cake 41
   24 - Peach Butter Pecan Dump Cake 43
   25 - Peach Strawberry Dump Cake 44
   26 - Blackberries vs Peaches Dump Cake 45

27 - Peach Delight Dump Cake 47
Pineapple 48
   28 - Strawberry Pineapple Layer Dump Cake 49
   29 - Pineapple Cherry Dump Cake 51
   30 - Tropical Getaway Dump Cake 52
   31 - Cherry Pineapple Gluten Free Dump Cake 54
   32 - Sweet Southern Mud Dump Cake 55
   33 - Lush Cherry Pineapple Dump Cake 56
Other Fruit 57
   34 - Plum Delicious Dump Cake 59
   35 - Banana Split Supreme Dump Cake 61
   36 - Banana Extreme Dump Cake 62
   37 - Simple Pear Dump Cake 63
No Fruit 64
   38 - Coffee Cake Dump Cake 65
   39 - Butterscotch Dump Cake 67
   40 - Incredible, Incredibly Simple Dump Cake 68
Chocolate 69
   41 - Salty Sweet Caramel-Chocolate Dump Cake 71
   42 - Creamy Chocolate Pudding Dump Cake 72
   43 - Slow Cooker White Chocolate Cherry Dump Cake 73
   44 - Sour Cream Chocolate Chip Dump Cake 74
Pumpkin 75
   45 - Pecan Pumpkin Dump Cake 77
   46 - Graham Pumpkin Dump Cake 78
   47 - Spiced Pumpkin Pie Dump Cake 79
   48 - Macadamia Pumpkin Dump Cake 80
Rhubarb 81
   49 - Light Strawberry Rhubarb Dump Cake 83
   50 - Rhuberry Dump Cake 84
   51 - Old Fashioned Rhubarb Dump Cake 85
Thank You 87
Other Books by Brianne Heaton 87
About the Author – Brianne Heaton 89
Connect with Brianne Heaton 90

Introduction

Baking doesn't have to be difficult or intimidating. You can make a delicious cake in just a few steps, with just a few ingredients by using a "dump" cake recipe. Dump cakes make less mess than traditional cakes and offer unusual and decadent choices that will wow those fortunate enough to have a bite. You'll find yourself trying incredible new combinations like salted caramel chocolate and cherry pineapple, as well as old favorites like Black Forest and chocolate chip.

All of these recipes are based around cake mixes, which allows you to tailor each recipe to your own taste by using whatever brand of mix you prefer be it organic or low sugar varieties. Most recipes also offer you the ability to make other changes easily to suit your own personal tastes, creating cakes that are distinctly your own.

Dump cake recipes can be used for all sorts of occasions. When you find yourself short of time and fancy ingredients, you can always throw together a dump cake for dessert. No one will know that you baked such a fabulous cake in the spur of the moment. You can even let the kids help out. Most of the recipes do not require mixing of ingredients in a separate bowl - they're both mixed and baked in the same dish! Mixing to baking to serving can often be done without dirtying up any extra dishes.

The people who eat your cakes won't believe that you made these yourself, and you won't believe how easy it was for you to pull them together!

Scrumptious Desserts To Satisfy Your Sweet Tooth

Apple

Scrumptious Desserts To Satisfy Your Sweet Tooth

1 - Apple Pie Dump Cake

An old fashioned taste of Americana, no one will be able to resist this cake once the aroma fills your home.

Ingredients:

- 1 cup (240 ml) butter or margarine
- 18.25 oz (500 g) yellow box cake mix
- 2 x 21 oz (588 g each) cans apple pie filling

Directions:

1. Turn the oven to 350°F (180°C).
2. Pull out a 9x13 inch (22.5x32.5 cm) glass or metal baking dish.
3. Pour the apple pie filling into the bottom of the dish.
4. Spread the dry cake mix evenly over the filling, being sure not to leave any clumps of powder.
5. Slice the butter or margarine and place across the top of the powder. DO NOT MIX.

6. Bake for 50 minutes, or slightly longer if using a glass dish, until the top is golden brown.
7. Serve warm.

2 - Blueberry Apple Dump Cake

This combination is delicious if not unexpected. The apples are bold and the blueberries sweet; the flavors of apple and blueberry somehow stand out separately in this amazing dessert.

Ingredients:

- ½ teaspoon (2.5 ml) cinnamon
- 1 tablespoon (15 ml) flour
- 1 tablespoon (15 ml) butter
- 1 cup (240 ml) blueberries - fresh or frozen
- 18.25 oz (500 g) yellow cake mix
- 6 medium apples, sliced thinly

Directions:

1. Turn the oven to 350°F (180°C).
2. Grease a 9x13 inch (22.5x32.5 cm) glass or metal baking dish.
3. Pour in the apple, topping off with the flour and cinnamon. Mix slightly.
4. Add the blueberries. Do not thaw the blueberries if using the frozen ones.
5. Spread the dry cake mix evenly over the filling, being sure not to leave any clumps of powder.
6. Slice the butter or margarine and place across the top of the powder. DO NOT MIX.
7. Bake for 60 minutes, or slightly longer if using a glass dish, until golden brown and bubbly.
8. Cool and serve.

3 - Golden Dump Cake

This cake is perfect on a brisk fall morning, or any time you want to throw yourself into the feeling of autumn. Be careful not to use pie filling or else your cake will fall apart.

Ingredients:

- ½ cup (120 ml) margarine or butter, melted
- ½ cup (120 ml) chopped pecans
- 18.25 oz (500 g) Spice cake mix
- 2 cans (20 oz or 560 g each) sliced apples, undrained - not pie filling!

Directions:

1. Turn the oven to 375°F (190°C).
2. Pull out a 9x13 inch (22.5x32.5 cm) glass or metal baking dish.
3. Pour the apples in the bottom of the pan, spreading evenly.
4. Spread the dry cake mix evenly over the apples, being sure not to leave any clumps of powder.
5. Pour the melted butter or margarine across the top of the powder.
6. Sprinkle with pecans. DO NOT MIX.
7. Bake for 40 minutes, or slightly longer if using a glass dish, until golden brown and bubbly.
8. Serve while warm with ice cream.

4 - Spiced Apple Pecan Dump Cake

A taste of fall that you can have any time of the year thanks to readily available canned apple pie filling. The spices are aromatic and absolutely divine.

Ingredients:

- ¼ teaspoon (1.25 ml) allspice
- ½ teaspoon (2.5 ml) nutmeg
- 1 teaspoon (5 ml) cinnamon
- ¾ cup (180 ml) margarine or butter
- 1 ½ cups (360 ml) chopped pecans
- 18.25 oz (500 g) box butter pecan cake mix
- 2 cans (21 oz or 588 g) apple pie filling

Directions:

1. Turn the oven to 350°F (180°C).
2. Pull out a 9x13 inch (22.5x32.5 cm) glass or metal baking dish.
3. Mix the spices in a small bowl.
4. Pour the apple filling into the prepared dish and spread evenly, then sprinkle with spices.
5. Spread the dry cake mix evenly over the filling, being sure not to leave any clumps of powder.
6. Place slices of the butter or margarine across the top of the powder, then sprinkle with pecans. DO NOT MIX.
7. Bake for 45-60 minutes, or slightly longer if using a glass dish, until golden brown and bubbling.
8. Allow to cool and serve with ice cream.

5 - Homemade French Apple Dump Cake

If you think of cake mixes as a mystery, allow this recipe to show you that there's not such secret stuff in that little box. Delicious and lovely.

Ingredients:

- 3 tablespoons (45 ml) Homemade Cake Mix
- 5 tablespoons (75 ml) butter
- ½ cup (120 ml) finely chopped pecans
- 21 oz (588 g) can apple pie filling
- 2 eggs

For the Homemade Cake Mix

- ½ teaspoon (2.5 ml) salt
- 1 teaspoon (5 ml) baking powder
- ¾ cup (180 ml) brown sugar
- 1 ½ cups (360 ml) flour

Directions:

1. Turn the oven to 350°F (180°C).
2. Pull out a 9x13 inch (22.5x32.5 cm) glass or metal baking dish.
3. Pour the apple pie filling into the prepared dish and spread evenly.
4. Blend 3 tablespoons (45 ml) homemade cake mix, eggs and 2 tablespoons (30 ml) of butter together. Whisk for 15 seconds.
5. Spread the mix over the fruit.
6. Spread the rest of the dry cake mix evenly over the filling, being sure not to leave any clumps of powder.
7. Sprinkle the pecans evenly across.
8. Place 3 tablespoons (45 ml) of chopped up cold butter across the top of the powder. DO NOT MIX.
9. Bake for 50 minutes, or slightly longer if using a glass dish, until golden brown.

10. Allow to cool and serve.

6 - Cinnamon Apple Dump Cake

This tasty treat is almost like an apple pie, with a wonderfully homecooked feel.

Ingredients:

- 1 tablespoon (15 ml) ground cinnamon
- ½ cup (120 ml) butter or margarine, melted
- 1 cup (240 ml) quick oats
- 18.25 oz (500 g) yellow cake mix
- 32 ounce (896 g) apple pie filling

Directions:

1. Turn the oven to 350°F (180°C).
2. Grease a 9x13 inch (22.5x32.5 cm) glass or metal baking dish.
3. Pour the apple filling into the prepared dish and spread evenly.
4. Spread the dry cake mix and oats evenly over the filling, being sure not to leave any clumps of powder.
5. Drizzle the melted butter or margarine across the top, followed by a sprinkling of cinnamon. DO NOT MIX.
6. Bake for 15-20 minutes, or slightly longer if using a glass dish, until golden brown and bubbly.
7. Allow to cool completely and serve with ice cream or whipped cream.

Berries

Scrumptious Desserts To Satisfy Your Sweet Tooth

7 - Everything Berry Dump Cake

Mixed berry is the name of the game. The tart and sweet flavors of this cake just melt together. The pecans offer some unexpected but worthwhile crunch to the chaos.

Ingredients:

- ½ cup (120 ml) unsalted butter, melted
- ¾ cup (180 ml) sugar
- 1 cup (240 ml) chopped pecans
- 1 cup (240 ml) blackberries
- 2 cups (480 ml) blueberries
- 2 cups (480 ml) raspberries
- 18.25 oz (500 g) box vanilla cake mix

Directions:

1. Turn the oven to 325°F (170°C).
2. Rinse the berries and dump them into a 9x13 inch (22.5x32.5 cm) glass or metal baking dish, spreading evenly.
3. Sprinkle the sugar across the berries.
4. Spread the dry cake mix evenly over the filling, being sure not to leave any clumps of powder.
5. Sprinkle the chopped pecans across the top.
6. Pour the melted butter evenly over the pan. DO NOT MIX.
7. Bake for 60 minutes, or slightly longer if using a glass dish, until the top is golden brown and the berries are bubbling.
8. Serve warm.

8 - Double Blackberry Dump Cake

This cake is beautiful as well as delicious. Bake it in a glass pan to show off the contrasting colors of the fresh berries and fluffy cake mix.

Ingredients:

- 1/3 cup (80 ml) sugar
- 1 box (3 oz or 84 g) blackberry or raspberry gelatin
- ½ cup (120 ml) chopped pecans (optional)
- 1 cup (240 ml) water
- 1 cup (240 ml) butter or margarine, melted
- 18.25 oz (500 g) yellow cake mix
- 4 cups (960 ml) fresh blackberries

Directions:

1. Turn the oven to 350°F (180°C).
2. Pull out a 9x13 inch (22.5x32.5 cm) glass or metal baking dish.
3. Place the berries in the bottom of the dish, spreading evenly.
4. Mix the gelatin and sugar together and sprinkle evenly over the berries.
5. Spread the dry cake mix evenly over the filling, being sure not to leave any clumps of powder.
6. Sprinkle the pecans over top.
7. Pour the melted butter or margarine across the top of the powder, followed by the water. DO NOT MIX.
8. Bake for 35-45 minutes, or slightly longer if using a glass dish, until an inserted toothpick comes out dry. The top should be a golden brown.
9. Allow to cool and serve with ice cream or whipped cream.

9 - Blueberry Lemon Dump Cake

This cake reminds me of a morning muffin, but sweeter and full of gooey goodness. Delicious with a cup of coffee

Ingredients:

- 3 tablespoons (45 ml) butter, thinly sliced
- 1 bag (about 12 oz or 336 g) frozen blueberries
- 18.25 oz (500 g) lemon cake mix
- 1 can (15 oz or 420 g) crushed pineapple, undrained

Directions:

1. Turn the oven to 350°F (180°C).
2. Pull out a 9x13 inch (22.5x32.5 cm) glass or metal baking dish.
3. Pour the berries, then the pineapple into the dish and spread evenly, mixing slightly.
4. Spread the dry cake mix evenly over the filling, being sure not to leave any clumps of powder.
5. Slice the butter or margarine and place across the top of the powder. DO NOT MIX.
6. Bake for 60 minutes, or slightly longer if using a glass dish, until golden brown and bubbly.
7. Serve after cooling for 15 minutes.

10 - Crumbly Blackberry Dump Cake

This cake will remind you of a tart or fruit pie. If you've never tried a cake made with fresh berries, then you must give this one a go.

Ingredients:

- 1 teaspoon (5 ml) ground cinnamon
- ½ cup (120 ml) white sugar
- ½ cup (120 ml) rolled oats
- 1 cup (240 ml) butter or margarine, melted
- 18.25 oz (500 g) box yellow cake mix
- 4 cups (960 ml) fresh blackberries

Directions:

1. Turn the oven to 350°F (180°C).
2. Pull out a 9x13 inch (22.5x32.5 cm) glass or metal baking dish.

3. Pour the berries, sugar and cinnamon into the bottom of the dish, mixing just a bit to combine.
4. Spread the dry cake mix and oats evenly over the filling, being sure not to leave any clumps of powder.
5. Pour the melted butter evenly over the pan. DO NOT MIX.
6. Bake for 30 minutes, or slightly longer if using a glass dish, until the top is golden brown and the berries are bubbling.
7. Serve warm with ice cream or whipped cream.

11 - Raspberry Vanilla Dump Cake

Raspberries have a bad reputation for being tart and sour, but this cake is sweet with an unusual kick of that sparkling raspberry flavor.

Ingredients:

- ½ cup (120 ml) butter or margarine, melted
- ½ cup (120 ml) sugar
- 4 cups (960 ml) frozen raspberries
- 18.25 oz (500 g) Vanilla Cake Mix

Directions:

1. Thaw raspberries overnight.
2. Turn the oven to 350°F (180°C).
3. Grease a 9x13 inch (22.5x32.5 cm) glass or metal baking dish.
4. Pour the raspberries and sugar into the prepared dish and spread evenly.
5. Spread the dry cake mix evenly over the filling, being sure not to leave any clumps of powder.
6. Pour the melted butter or margarine across the top of the powder. DO NOT MIX.
7. Bake for 3-45 minutes, or slightly longer if using a glass dish, until golden brown.
8. Allow to cool and serve with ice cream.

12 - Crunchy Blueberry Dump Cake

This cake will surprise you with its crunch. There is such an amazing mix of flavor and texture that you won't be able to have just one piece!

Ingredients:

- 1 tablespoon (15 ml) butter or margarine, melted
- ½ cup (120 ml) butter or margarine, melted
- ¾ cup (180 ml) sugar
- 1 cup (240 ml) chopped pecans
- 10 ounces (280 g) blueberries
- 18.25 oz (500 g) box yellow cake mix
- 21 oz (588 g) can crushed pineapple, undrained

Directions:

1. Turn the oven to 350°F (180°C).
2. Mix the blueberries, 1 tablespoon (15 ml) melted butter or margarine, and sugar in a bowl.
3. Grease a 9x13 inch (22.5x32.5 cm) glass or metal baking dish.
4. Pour the pineapple into the prepared dish and spread evenly.
5. Pour the blueberry mixture over pineapple, don't mix.
6. Spread the dry cake mix evenly over the filling, being sure not to leave any clumps of powder.
7. Pour the melted butter (½ cup or 120 ml) or margarine across the top of the powder, then sprinkle with pecans. DO NOT MIX.
8. Bake for 45-55 minutes, or slightly longer if using a glass dish, until golden brown.
9. Allow to cool and serve with ice cream or whipped cream.

13 - Fresh Blueberry Dump Cake

Plump and delicious, nothing beats a fresh blueberry cake. If you live in an area where you can pick the berries yourself, you can turn this cake into a full day of family fun.

Ingredients:

- 1 teaspoon (5 ml) ground cinnamon
- ½ cup (120 ml) white sugar
- ½ cup (120 ml) butter, melted
- 18.25 oz (500 g) box yellow cake mix
- 4 cups (960 ml) fresh blueberries

Directions:

1. Turn the oven to 350°F (180°C).
2. Pull out a 9x13 inch (22.5x32.5 cm) glass or metal baking dish.

3. Mix the berries, cinnamon and sugar in the bottom of the dish, spreading evenly.
4. Spread the dry cake mix evenly over the filling, being sure not to leave any clumps of powder.
5. Pour the melted butter evenly over the pan. DO NOT MIX.
6. Bake for 30 minutes, or slightly longer if using a glass dish, until the top is golden brown.
7. Serve warm or cool, topped with ice cream.

Cherry

Scrumptious Desserts To Satisfy Your Sweet Tooth

14 - Cherry Angel Dump Cake

Angel food is light and fluffy, the perfect complement to the gooey pineapple and chewy cherries.

Ingredients:

- 8 oz can (224 g) crushed pineapple in juice
- 1 can (14.5 oz or 411 gm) red tart cherries
- 18.25 oz (500 g) angel food cake mix

Directions:

1. Turn the oven to 350°F (180°C).
2. Grease a 9x13 inch (22.5x32.5 cm) glass or metal baking dish.
3. In a large bowl, mix the cake mix with a quarter cup (60 ml) cherry juice with a whisk, thoroughly combining for one minute.
4. Add in the pineapple and cherries along with the juices by folding into the batter.
5. Pour into the prepared dish and spread evenly,
6. Bake for 35-47 minutes, or slightly longer if using a glass dish, until golden brown. Be sure not to undercook.
7. Allow to cool slightly and serve.

15 - Cherry Crock Pot Dump Cake

Because this cake cooks for so long, the flavors practically melt together. The cherries blend into the moist delicious batter.

Ingredients:

- ½ cup (120 ml) butter or margarine, melted
- ½ cup (120 ml) walnuts (optional)
- 18.25 oz (500 g) yellow cake mix
- 21 oz (588 g) can cherry pie Filling

Directions:

1. Pour the cherry filling into a medium greased crock pot.
2. Combine the cake mix and butter or margarine in a separate bowl until crumbly.
3. Spread over the cherry filling.
4. Sprinkle with walnuts as an additional option.
5. Cook on the low setting for 4 hours or on the high setting for 2 hours.
6. Serve warm with ice cream.

16 - Cherry Pineapple Dump Cake

This cake is sweet and deliciously chewy. It goes well with almost any meal.

Ingredients:

- ½ cup (120 ml) butter or margarine, melted
- 8 oz (224 g) chopped walnuts
- 15 oz (420 g) can crushed pineapple
- 18.25 oz (500 g) box yellow cake mix
- 21 oz (588 g) can cherry pie filling

Directions:

1. Turn the oven to 350°F (180°C).
2. Pull out a 9x13 inch (22.5x32.5 cm) glass or metal baking dish.
3. Pour the pineapple and cherry pie filling into the bottom of the dish, mixing just a bit to combine.

4. Spread the dry cake mix evenly over the filling, being sure not to leave any clumps of powder.
5. Sprinkle the chopped walnuts across the top.
6. Pour the melted butter evenly over the pan. DO NOT MIX.
7. Bake for 35 to 40 minutes, or slightly longer if using a glass dish, until the top is golden brown.
8. Serve warm.

17 - Nutty Cherry Dump Cake

Coconut and cherry may seem like an odd combination, but the textures and flavors of this unusual cake come together perfectly. A great cake to take to a potluck, where it won't last long.

Ingredients:

- 8 oz (224 g) can crushed pineapple
- 1 cup (240 ml) chopped pecans
- 1 cup (240 ml) butter or margarine, melted
- 1 cup (240 ml) unsweetened shredded coconut
- 15 oz (420 g) can cherry pie filling
- 18.25 oz (500 g) yellow cake mix

Directions:

1. Turn the oven to 350°F (180°C).
2. Grease a 9x13 inch (22.5x32.5 cm) glass or metal baking dish.
3. Pour the fruit into the prepared dish and spread evenly.
4. Spread the dry cake mix evenly over the filling, being sure not to leave any clumps of powder.
5. Pour the melted butter or margarine across the top of the powder, then sprinkle with nuts and coconut. DO NOT MIX.
6. Bake for 55-65 minutes, or slightly longer if using a glass dish, until golden brown and an inserted toothpick comes out clean.
7. Allow to cool and serve with ice cream.

18 - Dark Cherry Black Forest Dump Cake

The combination of dark cherries and chocolate is nearly magical in this delicious and decadent sweet.

Ingredients:

- ¾ cup (180 ml) butter or margarine, cut into pats
- 1 cup (240 ml) chopped walnuts
- 15 oz (420 g) can pitted dark sweet cherries
- 18.25 oz (500 g) package chocolate cake mix
- 21 oz (588 g) can cherry pie filling

Directions:

1. Turn the oven to 375°F (190°C).
2. Grease a 9x13 inch (22.5x32.5 cm) glass or metal baking dish.
3. Pour the cherry pie filling into the prepared dish and spread evenly.
4. Spread the cherries and its juice across without mixing them in.
5. Spread the dry cake mix evenly over the filling, being sure not to leave any clumps of powder.
6. Sprinkle with walnuts then place the pats of butter or margarine across the top of the powder. DO NOT MIX.
7. Bake for 45 minutes, or slightly longer if using a glass dish, until golden brown.
8. Allow to cool and serve with ice cream.

19 - Cherry Choco Cola Dump Cake

Soda in the batter gives a fluffiness to this creation. Imagine a fluffy cloud of chocolate covered in cherries and you'll have an idea of how mouth watering this cake is.

Ingredients:

- 1 cup (240 ml) cola flavored soda
- 16 oz (448 g) maraschino cherries with juice, without stems
- 18.25 oz (500 g) box devil's food cake mix

Directions:

1. Turn the oven to 350°F (180°C).
2. Pull out a 9x13 inch (22.5x32.5 cm) glass or metal baking dish.
3. Pour the cherries with juice into the pan.
4. Whisk together the cake mix and soda in a large bowl.
5. Pour the mix over the cherries.
6. Bake 35-40 minutes, until an inserted toothpick comes out clean.

7. Allow the cake to cool for 15 minutes.
8. Cut and serve.

Citrus

Scrumptious Desserts To Satisfy Your Sweet Tooth

20 - Mandarin Dump Cake

Those little yellow oranges are so delicious right out of the can, but when mixed up in this recipe, you'll find that you love them even more.

Ingredients:

For the Cake

- 2 tablespoons (30 ml) flour
- ½ cup (120 ml) oil
- 15 oz (420 g) can mandarin oranges, undrained
- 18.25 oz (500 g) yellow cake mix
- 4 eggs

For the Topping

- 8 oz (224 g) whipped cream
- 8 oz (224 g) instant French vanilla dry pudding mix
- 15 oz (420 g) can crushed pineapple, undrained

Directions:

1. Turn the oven to 350°F (180°C).
2. Pull out a 9x13 inch (22.5x32.5 cm) glass or metal baking dish.
3. Mix the flour, oil, eggs, oranges and cake mix in a large bowl, stirring vigorously for two minutes.
4. Pour into prepared dish.
5. Bake for 30-40 minutes, or slightly longer if using a glass dish, until an inserted toothpick comes out clean.
6. Cool completely.
7. Mix the whipped cream, dry pudding mix and pineapple.
8. Spread over the cake and serve immediately.

21 - Lemon Delight Dump Cake

You won't believe how amazing lemon can taste until you've tried this recipe. Tart and sweet all at once, it's absolutely perfect.

Ingredients:

For the Cake
- 3 oz (84 g) lemon pudding mix
- ½ cup (120 ml) oil
- 1 cup (240 ml) water
- 18.25 oz (500 g) yellow cake mix
- 4 eggs

For the Frosting
- ½ teaspoon (2.5 ml) vanilla
- ½ teaspoon (2.5 ml) lemon extract
- 1 tablespoon (15 ml) milk
- ½ cup (120 ml) butter or margarine
- 1 box (1 lb or 450 g) confectioners' sugar

Directions:
1. Turn the oven to 350°F (180°C).
2. Grease a 9x13 inch (22.5x32.5 cm) glass or metal baking dish.
3. Mix the oil, water, eggs, pudding mix and cake mix in a large bowl, stirring vigorously for two minutes.
4. Bake for 40 minutes, or slightly longer if using a glass dish, until an inserted toothpick comes out clean.
5. Cool completely.
6. Beat together the butter or margarine, confectioners' sugar, milk, vanilla and lemon extract for two minutes.
7. Spread over the cake and serve immediately.

22 - Chocolate Orange Surprise Dump Cake

The surprise in this cake is the combination of oranges and cherries. Together they are sweet and tart, melting in your mouth.

Ingredients:

- 5 tablespoons (75 ml) butter or margarine softened and cut into dots
- 9 oz (252 g) chocolate cake mix
- 16 oz (448 g) cherry pie filling
- 16 oz (448 g) mandarin oranges, drained

Directions:

1. Turn the oven to 350°F (180°C).
2. Pull out a 9x13 inch (22.5x32.5 cm) glass or metal baking dish.
3. Pour the cherry pie filling into the prepared dish and spread evenly.
4. Spread the dry cake mix evenly over the filling, being sure not to leave any clumps of powder.
5. Now spread the mandarin oranges across evenly.
6. Dot the butter or margarine across the top of fruit. DO NOT MIX.
7. Bake for 30-40 minutes, or slightly longer if using a glass dish, until golden brown.
8. Allow to cool completely and serve with ice cream or whipped cream.

Scrumptious Desserts To Satisfy Your Sweet Tooth

Peach

23 - Southern Style Peach Dump Cake

This sweet treat will make you think you've died and gone to heaven. The peaches retain their texture, but each bite just melts in your mouth.

Ingredients:

- ¾ cup (180 ml) butter or margarine, sliced thinly, plus a bit more to grease the baking dish
- 18.25 oz (500 g) box yellow cake mix
- 29 oz (800 g) can sliced peaches in syrup, undrained

Directions:

1. Turn the oven to 350°F (180°C).
2. Grease a 9x13 inch (22.5x32.5 cm) glass or metal baking dish.
3. Pour the peaches and syrup into the bottom of the greased dish.
4. Spread the dry cake mix evenly over the peaches, being sure not to leave any clumps of powder.

5. Arrange the sliced butter or margarine across the top of the powder.
6. Bake 35 to 40 minutes, or slightly longer if using a glass dish, until the top is golden brown.
7. Serve warm.

24 - Peach Butter Pecan Dump Cake

Peaches are always delicious, but combined with the buttery cake mix and chewy coconut they are absolutely divine.

Ingredients:

- ¾ cup (180 ml) butter or margarine, melted
- 1 cup (240 ml) flaked coconut
- 1 cup (240 ml) chopped pecans
- 18.25 oz (500 g) Butter Pecan cake mix
- 1 can (29 oz or 812 g) sliced peaches in syrup, undrained

Directions:

1. Turn the oven to 350°F (180°C).
2. Pull out a 9x13 inch (22.5x32.5 cm) glass or metal baking dish.
3. Pour the peaches with its juice into the dish and spread evenly,
4. Spread the dry cake mix evenly over the filling, being sure not to leave any clumps of powder.
5. Spread the coconut and pecans across the top of the cake mix.
6. Pour the melted butter or margarine across the top of the powder. DO NOT MIX.
7. Bake for 45-55 minutes, or slightly longer if using a glass dish, until an inserted toothpick comes out clean.
8. Allow to cool slightly for 15 minutes and serve with ice cream.

25 - Peach Strawberry Dump Cake

This cake tastes absolutely like summertime. Fresh and joyful, this is the kind of cake that melts in your mouth.

Ingredients:

- 1/3 teaspoon (1.7 ml) cinnamon
- ½ teaspoon (2.5 ml) salt
- 2 tablespoons (30 ml) flour
- 1/3 cup (80 ml) butter, melted
- ½ cup (120 ml) sugar
- 2 cups (480 ml) strawberries, hulled and quartered
- ½ box (9 oz or 450 g) butter cake mix
- 4 peaches peeled and sliced

Directions:

1. Turn the oven to 350°F (180°C).
2. Grease a 9x13 inch (22.5x32.5 cm) glass or metal baking dish.
3. Pour the peaches, strawberries, sugar and flour into the prepared dish and spread evenly, mixing slightly.
4. Spread the dry cake mix evenly over the filling, being sure not to leave any clumps of powder.
5. Pour the melted butter or margarine across the top of the powder. DO NOT MIX.
6. Bake for 60 minutes, or slightly longer if using a glass dish, until golden brown.
7. Sprinkle salt and cinnamon over top.
8. Serve with ice cream or with whipped cream after cooling for 15 minutes.

26 - Blackberries vs Peaches Dump Cake

This cake tastes like an epic battle between sweet and sweetly tart. The flavors complement each other unexpectedly. Go out on a limb and try it!

Ingredients:

- 1 tsp (5 ml) cinnamon (optional)
- ¾ cup (180 ml) butter or margarine, melted
- ¾ cup (180 ml) chopped pecans
- 18.25 oz (500 g) box yellow cake mix
- 21 oz (588 g) can peach pie filling
- 21 oz (588 g) can blackberry pie filling

Directions:

1. Turn the oven to 350°F (180°C).
2. Pull out a 9x13 inch (22.5x32.5 cm) glass or metal baking dish.

3. Pour the two pie fillings into the bottom of the dish and sprinkle in the cinnamon. Mix evenly to combine.
4. Spread the dry cake mix evenly over the filling, being sure not to leave any clumps of powder.
5. Sprinkle with the pecans.
6. Pour the melted butter evenly over the pan. DO NOT MIX.
7. Bake for 45 minutes, or slightly longer if using a glass dish, until the top is golden brown and the berries are bubbling.
8. Serve warm with whipped cream or with ice cream.

27 - Peach Delight Dump Cake

This cake is so sweet and gooey that it will satisfy the most intense sweet tooth.

Ingredients:

- 2 tablespoons (30 ml) butter or margarine
- 15 oz (420 g) can crushed pineapple
- 18.25 oz (500 g) yellow cake mix
- 29 oz (812 g) can sliced peaches

Directions:

1. Turn the oven to 350°F (180°C).
2. Grease a 9x13 inch (22.5x32.5 cm) glass or metal baking dish.
3. Pour the fruit into the prepared dish and spread evenly.
4. Spread the dry cake mix evenly over the filling, being sure not to leave any clumps of powder.
5. Chop the butter or margarine and place across the top of the powder. DO NOT MIX.
6. Bake for 45-50 minutes, or slightly longer if using a glass dish, until golden brown.
7. Allow to cool and serve with ice cream.

Scrumptious Desserts To Satisfy Your Sweet Tooth

Pineapple

28 - Strawberry Pineapple Layer Dump Cake

This one is almost criminal. The pineapple is sticky and gooey, while the strawberries offer you a fresh taste that reminds you of summer.

Ingredients:

- 1 cup (240 ml) butter or margarine
- 1 cup (240 ml) nuts, chopped
- 15 oz (420 g) can crushed pineapple with juice
- 15 oz (420 g) can strawberry pie filling
- 18.25 oz (500 g) box yellow cake mix

Directions:

1. Turn the oven to 325°F (170°C).
2. Grease a 9x13 inch (22.5x32.5 cm) glass or metal baking dish.
3. Pour the pineapple into the bottom of the dish, spreading evenly.
4. Spread the pie filling over the pineapple evenly.

5. Spread the dry cake mix evenly over the filling, being sure not to leave any clumps of powder.
6. Slice the butter or margarine and place across the top of the powder. DO NOT MIX.
7. Bake for 45 minutes, or slightly longer if using a glass dish, until the top is golden brown.
8. Allow to cool and serve right from the pan.

29 - Pineapple Cherry Dump Cake

Between the cherries and the pineapple, this cake almost tastes like it came from a candy shop. It begs to be eaten with a spoon instead of a fork.

Ingredients:

- ¼ cup (60 ml) butter or margarine
- 1 can (15 oz or 420 g) crushed pineapple
- 18.25 oz (500 g) box of vanilla cake mix
- 1 can (21 oz or 588 g) cherry pie filling

Directions:

1. Turn the oven to 350°F (180°C).
2. Pull out a 9x13 inch (22.5x32.5 cm) glass or metal baking dish.
3. Layer the cherries, then the pineapple onto the bottom of the pan, spreading evenly.
4. Spread the dry cake mix evenly over the pineapple, being sure not to leave any clumps of powder.
5. Slice the butter and place across the top of the powder. DO NOT MIX.
6. Bake for 20-25 minutes, or slightly longer if using a glass dish, until golden brown and bubbly.
7. Serve while warm with ice cream or whipped cream.

30 - Tropical Getaway Dump Cake

You've never had a cake like this. A taste of the Pacific, brimming with exotic fruit flavors, this cake is a sumptuous delight.

Ingredients:

- 2 tablespoons (30 ml) cornstarch
- 2 tablespoons (30 ml) sugar
- ½ cup (120 ml) instant oatmeal
- 10 oz (300 ml) butter or margarine
- 15 oz (420 g) can tropical fruit mix
- 18.25 oz (500 g) package orange cake mix
- 21 oz (588 g) can cubed or crushed pineapple

Directions:

1. Turn the oven to 350°F (180°C).
2. Put the tropical fruit mix and 1/3 of the pineapple juice together in a bowl.
3. Mix in sugar with the juice mixture.
4. Put juice mixture in a small pan over low to medium heat and add 2 tablespoons (30 ml) butter. When bubbling, add the cornstarch, whisking until smooth and thick.
5. Grease a 9x13 inch (22.5x32.5 cm) glass or metal baking dish.
6. Pour the fruit and remaining juice into the prepared dish and spread evenly.
7. Pour the cornstarch juice mix over the top.
8. Spread the dry cake mix evenly over the filling, being sure not to leave any clumps of powder.
9. Sprinkle the oatmeal over the top, crumbling in with your fingers.
10. Pour the melted butter or margarine across the top of the powder. DO NOT MIX.
11. Bake for 60 minutes, or slightly longer if using a glass dish, until golden brown.

12. Allow to cool and serve with ice cream.

31 - Cherry Pineapple Gluten Free Dump Cake

Who says that gluten free can't be delicious? This cake takes a normal gluten free mix and transforms it into a delectable treat.

Ingredients:

- ½ cup (120 ml) butter or margarine, sliced into ¼ inch (0.6 cm) thin pats
- 2 cans (15 oz or 420 g) dark sweet cherries, drained
- 18.25 oz (500 g) box gluten free yellow cake mix
- 21 oz (588 g) can crushed pineapple

Directions:

1. Turn the oven to 350°F (180°C).
2. Grease a 9x13 inch (22.5x32.5 cm) glass or metal baking dish.
3. Layer the pineapple and pineapple juice then the cherries in the prepared dish and spread evenly.
4. Spread the dry cake mix evenly over the filling, being sure not to leave any clumps of powder.
5. Place butter or margarine across the top of the powder, then sprinkle with pecans and toffee. DO NOT MIX.
6. Bake for 45-60 minutes, or slightly longer if using a glass dish, until golden brown.
7. Allow to cool and serve with ice cream.

32 - Sweet Southern Mud Dump Cake

This cake is only for those with a sweet tooth who take their treats seriously. It's almost too much to handle, and yet will still have you coming back for seconds.

Ingredients:

- ½ cup (120 ml) mint chocolate chips
- ½ cup (120 ml) butter or margarine, sliced
- 1 cup (240 ml) chopped pecans
- 18.25 oz (500 g) package devil's food cake mix
- 21 oz (588 g) can crushed pineapple, undrained
- 21 oz (588 g) can cherry pie filling

Directions:

1. Turn the oven to 350°F (180°C).
2. Grease a 9x13 inch (22.5x32.5 cm) glass or metal baking dish and dust with flour.
3. Pour the pineapple along with its juice into the prepared dish and spread evenly, then spread the cherry filling over it, not mixing.
4. Spread the dry cake mix evenly over the filling, being sure not to leave any clumps of powder.
5. Sprinkle with pecans and chocolate chips then place butter or margarine across the top of the powder. DO NOT MIX.
6. Bake for 40 minutes, or slightly longer if using a glass dish, until golden brown and an inserted toothpick comes out clean.
7. Allow to cool and serve.

33 - Lush Cherry Pineapple Dump Cake

This marvelously exotic cake is simply delicious. The cherries and pineapple are a truly wonderful combination, offering homey and exotic tastes all in one.

Ingredients:

- 7 oz (196 g) package shredded coconut
- 1 cup (240 ml) melted butter or margarine
- 1 cup (240 ml) chopped macadamia nuts
- 18.25 oz (500 g) package yellow cake mix
- 21 oz (588 g) can cherry pie filling
- 21 oz (588 g) can crushed pineapple

Directions:

1. Turn the oven to 350°F (180°C).
2. Grease a 9x13 inch (22.5x32.5 cm) glass or metal baking dish.
3. Layer the pineapple and its juice, followed by the cherries in the prepared dish and spread evenly without stirring.
4. Spread the dry cake mix evenly over the filling, being sure not to leave any clumps of powder.
5. Pour the melted butter or margarine across the top of the powder, then sprinkle with coconut and nuts. DO NOT MIX.
6. Bake for 50-60 minutes, or slightly longer if using a glass dish, until golden brown.
7. Allow to cool for 30 minutes. Serve either warm or cold.

Other Fruit

Scrumptious Desserts To Satisfy Your Sweet Tooth

34 - Plum Delicious Dump Cake

Plum cake isn't exactly what we find everyday on the supermarket shelf, but the plums are lightly sweet and delicious in this cake.

Ingredients:

For the Cake
- 1 teaspoon (5 ml) ground cloves
- 1 teaspoon (5 ml) cinnamon
- ½ cup (120 ml) chopped walnuts
- ½ cup (120 ml) sugar
- 1 cup (240 ml) canola oil
- 18.25 oz (500 g) box yellow cake mix
- 2 jars (4.5 oz or 128 ml each) strained plum baby food
- 4 eggs

For the Glaze
- 1 cup (240 ml) confectioners' sugar
- Juice from 1 lemon

Directions:
1. Turn the oven to 350°F (180°C).
2. Grease and flour a 9x13 inch (22.5x32.5 cm) baking dish or a bundt pan.
3. Mix the wet cake ingredients and the dry cake ingredients in separate bowls.
4. Slowly add the dry ingredients to the wet, mixing with an electric mixer at medium speed, until well blended.
5. Pour into your prepared pan.
6. Bake until an inserted toothpick into the center comes out dry, 55-65 minutes.
7. While the cake bakes, mix the glaze ingredients together with a whisk.
8. Allow the cake to cool 15 minutes on a cooling rack before turning over.
9. Pour the glaze over the still warm cake and allow to cool completely before serving.

35 - Banana Split Supreme Dump Cake

Who doesn't love a banana split? This cake is fun and fanciful, and will take you back to the days of shared treats at the soda counter. Great one to make with kids!

Ingredients:

- ½ cup (120 ml) crushed nuts
- 1 cup (240 ml) coconut
- 18.25 oz (500 g) white cake mix, dry
- 21 oz (588 g) can strawberry pie filling
- 21 oz (588 g) can crushed pineapple, undrained
- ½ cup (120 ml) margarine, sliced
- 1 banana, sliced
- Chocolate syrup
- Whipped cream

Directions:

1. Turn the oven to 325°F (170°C).
2. Grease a 9x13 inch (22.5x32.5 cm) glass or metal baking dish.
3. Pour the strawberry filling into the prepared dish and spread evenly.
4. Pour the pineapple across and spread evenly, don't mix.
5. Spread the dry cake mix evenly over the filling, being sure not to leave any clumps of powder.
6. Pour the melted butter or margarine across the top of the powder, then sprinkle with nuts and coconut. DO NOT MIX.
7. Bake for 60-75 minutes, or slightly longer if using a glass dish, until golden brown.
8. Serve warm or cold with whipped cream, banana slices and chocolate syrup.

36 - Banana Extreme Dump Cake

The combination of cream cheese and sour cream in this cake along with the soft sweetness of the banana is perfectly balanced and will give you a tasty treat unlike anything you've had before.

Ingredients:

- 1 teaspoon (5 ml) baking powder
- 1 teaspoon (5 ml) baking soda
- 2 teaspoons (10 ml) vanilla
- ½ cup (120 ml) butter or margarine, softened
- 8 oz (224 g) cream cheese
- 1 cup (240 ml) bananas, mashed
- 1 cup (240 ml) sour cream
- 1 cup (240 ml) sugar
- 1 lb (450 g) confectioners' sugar
- 2 cups (480 ml) flour
- 2 eggs

Directions:

1. Turn the oven to 350°F (180°C).
2. Grease a 9x13 inch (22.5x32.5 cm) glass or metal baking dish.
3. In a large bowl, mix the sugar, butter or margarine, eggs, bananas, flour, baking soda, baking powder, half of the vanilla and sour cream with a spoon, thoroughly combining.
4. Pour into the prepared dish and spread evenly.
5. Bake for 40 minutes, or slightly longer if using a glass dish, until golden brown.
6. While it's baking, beat together the remaining vanilla, cream cheese and powdered sugar until smooth.
7. Allow to cool before applying the frosting
8. Serve as is.

37 - Simple Pear Dump Cake

This recipe is so simple and yet so delicious. The pears maintain their texture throughout the cooking, resulting in a dessert that is more similar to a decadent fruit tart than to a traditional fluffy cake.

Ingredients:

- ½ cup (120 ml) butter or margarine, melted
- 18.25 oz (500 g) yellow cake mix
- 21 oz (588 g) can sliced pears in heavy syrup
- Ground ginger or nutmeg

Directions:

1. Turn the oven to 350°F (180°C).
2. Pull out a 9x13 inch (22.5x32.5 cm) glass or metal baking dish.
3. Pour the fruit into the dish and spread evenly.
4. Spread the dry cake mix evenly over the filling, being sure not to leave any clumps of powder.
5. Pour the melted butter or margarine across the top of the powder, then sprinkle with ginger. DO NOT MIX.
6. Bake for 35 minutes, or until golden brown and bubbly.
7. Serve it up warm with a side of ice cream or whipped cream.

Scrumptious Desserts To Satisfy Your Sweet Tooth

No Fruit

38 - Coffee Cake Dump Cake

Brew a pot of great coffee and sit down with this heavy and filling spiced cake. It's so easy and yet so delicious that after you try it you'll never feel quite right about drinking coffee without a piece of this.

Ingredients:

For the Cake
- 1 teaspoon (5 ml) nutmeg
- 2 teaspoons (10 ml) baking powder
- 1/3 cup (80 ml) butter
- 1 cup (240 ml) sugar
- 1 cup (240 ml) milk
- 2 cups (480 ml) flour
- 1 egg
- Dash of salt

For the Topping
- 1 teaspoon (5 ml) cinnamon
- 1 tablespoon (15 ml) flour
- 2 tablespoons (30 ml) butter or margarine
- ½ cup (120 ml) sugar

Directions:
1. Turn the oven to 350°F (180°C).
2. Grease a 9x13 inch (22.5x32.5 cm) glass or metal baking dish and dust with flour.
3. Mix everything together except the topping ingredients in a large bowl with a whisk or mixer until smooth and completely combined.
4. Pour into prepared dish.

5. With a fork, mix the topping ingredients together then spread on top of the cake mixture.
6. Bake in the preheated oven for 20-30 minutes, until an inserted toothpick comes out clean.

39 - Butterscotch Dump Cake

Who says that butterscotch is reserved for pudding and candy? This recipe is the perfect mix of both and is a must try for butterscotch lovers.

Ingredients:

- 3 oz. (84 g) box cook and serve butterscotch pudding mix
- 1 cup (240 ml) chopped nuts
- 1 package (12 oz or 336 g) butterscotch chips
- 2 cups (480 ml) milk
- 18.25 oz (500 g) vanilla cake mix

Directions:

1. Turn the oven to 350°F (180°C).
2. Grease a 9x13 inch (22.5x32.5 cm) glass or metal baking dish and dust with flour.
3. Prepare the pudding with the milk and whisk for two minutes.
4. Stir in the cake mix, combining thoroughly. Batter will be very thick.
5. Pour into the prepared dish and spread evenly.
6. Scatter with nuts and butterscotch chips across the top.
7. Bake for 30-35 minutes, or slightly longer if using a glass dish, until the edges pull away from the sides and the butterscotch is melted, forming a frosting.
8. Serve warm or cool.

40 - Incredible, Incredibly Simple Dump Cake

This recipe is the best of the best and satisfies everyone's tastes. It's a recipe that you can tailor to your own taste, so choose your favorite - vanilla or chocolate. Or better yet, make one of each.

Ingredients:

- 1 teaspoon (5ml) cinnamon
- ¼ cup (60 ml) nuts of your choice
- 3 oz (84 g) vanilla or chocolate instant pudding
- ½ cup (120 ml) vegetable oil
- ½ cup (120 ml) brown sugar
- 1 cup (240 ml) sour cream
- 18.25 oz (500 g) yellow or chocolate cake mix
- 4 eggs

Directions:

1. Turn the oven to 350°F (180°C).
2. Grease a 9x13 inch (22.5x32.5 cm) glass or metal baking dish and dust with flour.
3. Mix all of the ingredients except for the cinnamon, sugar and nuts together to form a thick batter.
4. Spread evenly across the prepared pan.
5. Mix together remaining ingredients and sprinkle across the top of the batter.
6. Bake for 60 minutes, or slightly longer if using a glass dish, until golden brown.
7. Allow to cool completely and serve with ice cream or whipped cream.

Chocolate

Scrumptious Desserts To Satisfy Your Sweet Tooth

41 - Salty Sweet Caramel-Chocolate Dump Cake

Salt and sweet are tastes that our bodies crave. Mix them together in this cake to find yourself coming back again and again.

Ingredients:

- 1 small box (3.9 oz or 109 g) instant chocolate pudding
- 1 cup (240 ml) semi-sweet chocolate chips
- 1 ½ cups (360 ml) cold milk
- 1 ½ cups (360 ml) chopped caramels
- 18.25 oz (500 g) devil's food cake mix
- Sprinkling of coarse sea salt

Directions:

1. Turn the oven to 350°F (180°C).
2. Grease a 9x13 inch (22.5x32.5 cm) glass or metal baking dish.
3. Mix together the chocolate pudding and milk in a large bowl. Whisk for one minute.
4. Mix the cake mix and stir until combined.
5. Spread the thick batter evenly across the pan.
6. Sprinkle the caramels, then sea salt evenly across the batter.
7. Bake for 35-40 minutes, or slightly longer if using a glass dish, until an inserted toothpick comes out clean.
8. Microwave the chocolates on high for 2-3 minutes in a small bowl, stirring every 30 seconds, until melted.
9. Drizzle cooled cake with chocolate.
10. Serve warm or cool with whipped cream.

42 - Creamy Chocolate Pudding Dump Cake

This cake is creamy and moist straight out of the oven. Imagine a decadent light and smooth brownie, and you're close to this amazing dessert.

Ingredients:

- 3 oz (84 g) package chocolate pudding
- 1 ½ cups (360 ml) milk
- 1 ½ cups (360 ml) chocolate chips
- 18.25 oz (500 g) box chocolate cake mix

Directions:

1. Turn the oven to 350°F (180°C).
2. Pull out a 9x13 inch (22.5x32.5 cm) glass or metal baking dish.
3. Adding the milk to the pudding to prepare and whisk for two minutes.
4. Stir in the cake mix, combining thoroughly. The batter will be very thick.
5. Pour into the prepared dish and spread evenly.
6. Scatter with chocolate chips.
7. Bake the the cake for 30 minutes, or slightly longer if using a glass dish, until the edges pull away from the sides.
8. Serve warm or cool.

43 - Slow Cooker White Chocolate Cherry Dump Cake

No one will believe that this cake came from your slow cooker! And you won't believe how amazing your house smells while the white chocolate and cherries are cooking for hours.

Ingredients:

- ½ cup (120 ml) butter or margarine, melted
- 1 cup (240 ml) white chocolate chips
- 18.25 oz (500 g) box yellow cake mix
- 21 oz (588 g) can cherry pie filling

Directions:

1. Grease a large slow cooker (3.5 qt or 3.5L) with cooking spray.
2. Pour the cherry pie filling into the prepared cooker and spread evenly.
3. Spread the dry cake mix evenly over the filling, being sure not to leave any clumps of powder.
4. Pour the melted butter or margarine across the top of the powder, then sprinkle with white chocolate chips. DO NOT MIX.
5. Cook on high for 2.5-3 hours, until the middle is set.
6. Keep warm in the slow cooker until time to serve.
7. Serve with a scoop of ice cream.

44 - Sour Cream Chocolate Chip Dump Cake

The secret to this cake is the sour cream, which may seem small but gives it a savoriness that will have you coming back slice after slice.

Ingredients:

- ½ cup (120 ml) vegetable oil
- 1 cup (240 ml) sour cream
- 3 oz (84 g) package instant vanilla pudding
- 6 oz (168 g) chocolate chips
- 18.25 oz (500 g) box yellow cake mix
- 4 eggs

Directions:

1. Turn the oven to 350°F (180°C).
2. Grease a 9x13 inch (22.5x32.5 cm) glass or metal baking dish.
3. Mix the oil, eggs, sour cream, pudding and cake mix in a large bowl, stirring vigorously for three to four minutes.
4. Fold in the chocolate chips.
5. Pour into prepared dish.
6. Bake for 60 minutes, or slightly longer if using a glass dish, until an inserted toothpick comes out clean.
7. Cool completely and serve with ice cream or whipped cream.

Pumpkin

Scrumptious Desserts To Satisfy Your Sweet Tooth

45 - Pecan Pumpkin Dump Cake

The milk in this recipe lends a fullness and moist gooey quality to this delicious cake creation.

Ingredients:

- ½ cup (120 ml) butter or margarine, melted
- 1 cup (240 ml) canned evaporated milk
- 1 cup (240 ml) pecan halves
- 18.25 oz (500 g) yellow cake mix
- 1 large can (30 oz or 840 g) pumpkin pie mix
- 2 eggs

Directions:

1. Turn the oven to 350°F (180°C).
2. Pull out a 9x13 inch (22.5x32.5 cm) glass or metal baking dish.
3. In a large bowl, combine the pumpkin pie mix, eggs and milk thoroughly.
4. Pour into the dish and spread evenly,
5. Spread the dry cake mix evenly over the filling, being sure not to leave any clumps of powder.
6. Pour the melted butter or margarine across the top of the powder, then sprinkle with pecans. DO NOT MIX.
7. Bake for 45 minutes, or slightly longer if using a glass dish, until golden brown.
8. Allow to cool and serve with whipped cream.

46 - Graham Pumpkin Dump Cake

This cake is absolutely a must try. There are so many textures and flavors that your mouth won't quite know what to do! Smooth pumpkin, gooey toffee and crunchy crackers are a perfect combination.

Ingredients:

- 1 tablespoon (15 ml) pumpkin pie spice
- ½ cup (120 ml) toffee bits (optional)
- 1 cup (240 ml) coarsely crushed Graham crackers
- 1 cup (240 ml) butter or margarine, melted
- 1 cup (240 ml) light brown sugar
- 1 can (10 oz or 300 ml) canned evaporated milk
- 18.25 oz (500 g) yellow cake mix
- 1 small can (15 oz or 420 g) pumpkin puree
- 3 eggs

Directions:

1. Turn the oven to 350°F (180°C).
2. Grease a 9x13 inch (22.5x32.5 cm) glass or metal baking dish.
3. In a large bowl, mix the pumpkin puree, milk, eggs, sugar and pumpkin spice thoroughly.
4. Pour into the prepared dish and spread evenly.
5. Spread the dry cake mix evenly over the filling, being sure not to leave any clumps of powder.
6. Sprinkle the Graham crackers and toffee over top.
7. Pour the melted butter or margarine evenly across the top of the powder. DO NOT MIX.
8. Bake for 45-50 minutes, or slightly longer if using a glass dish, until golden brown.
9. Allow to cool and serve with ice cream.

47 - Spiced Pumpkin Pie Dump Cake

This is a great fall or winter cake, and will fill your home with smells that make your mouth water. It's dense, so be sure to try it with whipped cream.

Ingredients:

- 4 teaspoons (20 ml) pumpkin pie spice
- ¾ cup (180 ml) butter or margarine, melted
- 1 ½ cups (360 ml) finely chopped walnuts
- 1 can (14 oz or 420 ml) condensed milk
- 1 small can (15 oz or 420 g) pumpkin pie mix
- 18.25 oz (500 g) box spiced cake mix
- 3 eggs

Directions:

1. Turn the oven to 350°F (180°C).
2. Grease a 9x13 inch (22.5x32.5 cm) glass or metal baking dish.
3. In a large bowl, mix the pumpkin, milk, eggs and spice thoroughly.
4. Pour into the prepared dish and spread evenly.
5. Spread the dry cake mix evenly over the filling, being sure not to leave any clumps of powder.
6. Sprinkle with the walnuts then pour the melted butter or margarine across the top of the powder. DO NOT MIX.
7. Bake for 50 minutes, or slightly longer if using a glass dish, until golden brown.
8. Allow to cool slightly and serve with whipped cream or ice cream.

48 - Macadamia Pumpkin Dump Cake

This cake is dense and hearty, and the macadamia nuts offer a mouth-watering flavor that will wow the pickiest eater.

Ingredients:

- ½ teaspoon (2.5 ml) salt
- 1 teaspoon (5 ml) cinnamon
- 1 cup (240 ml) sweetened shredded coconut (optional)
- 1 cup (240 ml) butter, melted
- 12 oz (336 g) evaporated milk
- 1 ½ cups (360 ml) sugar
- 15 oz (420 g) pumpkin puree
- 2 cups (480 ml) macadamia nuts, finely chopped
- 18.25 oz (500 g) yellow cake mix
- 3 large eggs

Directions:

1. Turn the oven to 350°F (180°C).
2. Grease a 9x13 inch (22.5x32.5 cm) glass or metal baking dish.
3. In a large bowl, mix the pumpkin, sugar, eggs, cinnamon, salt, coconut and milk, thoroughly combining.
4. Pour into the prepared dish and spread evenly.
5. Spread the dry cake mix evenly over the filling, being sure not to leave any clumps of powder.
6. Sprinkle with nuts then pour the melted butter or margarine across the top of the nuts and powder. DO NOT MIX.
7. Bake for 50-55 minutes, or slightly longer if using a glass dish, until golden brown.
8. Allow to cool and serve.

Rhubarb

Scrumptious Desserts To Satisfy Your Sweet Tooth

49 - Light Strawberry Rhubarb Dump Cake

Fluffy and light, this cake twists it's flavors together beautifully. It comes together so easily!

Ingredients:

- 3 oz package (84 g) strawberry flavored gelatin
- ½ cup (120 ml) melted butter
- 1 cup (240 ml) sugar
- 1 ¼ cup (300 ml) water
- 4 cups (960 ml) chopped rhubarb
- 18.25 oz (500 g) yellow cake mix

Directions:

1. Turn the oven to 350°F (180°C).
2. Grease a 9x13 inch (22.5x32.5 cm) glass or metal baking dish.
3. Pour the rhubarb into the prepared dish and spread evenly.
4. Sprinkle the sugar and then the gelatin across the top.
5. Spread the dry cake mix evenly over the filling, being sure not to leave any clumps of powder.
6. Pour in the water slowly then add the melted butter or margarine across the top. DO NOT MIX.
7. Bake for 60 minutes, or slightly longer if using a glass dish, until an inserted toothpick comes out clean.
8. Serve warm or cool.

50 - Rhuberry Dump Cake

This cake tastes like nothing you've ever eaten before. The tartness of rhubarb balanced with the delicate sweetness of strawberries go so well together in this decadent piece.

Ingredients:

- 1 tablespoon (15 ml) lemon juice
- ½ cup (120 ml) butter or margarine, melted
- 1 ½ cups (360 ml) rhubarb, chopped into ½ inch (1.25 cm) pieces
- ½ box (9 oz or 450 g) yellow cake mix
- 1 can (16 oz or 448 g) strawberry pie filling
- Pinch of salt

Directions:

1. Turn the oven to 350°F (180°C).
2. Pull out a 9x13 inch (22.5x32.5 cm) glass or metal baking dish.
3. Pour in the rhubarb, strawberry pie filling, salt and lemon into the prepared dish and spread evenly, mixing slightly.
4. Spread the dry cake mix evenly over the filling, being sure not to leave any clumps of powder.
5. Pour the melted butter or margarine across the top of the powder. DO NOT MIX.
6. Bake for 35 minutes, or slightly longer if using a glass dish, until golden brown.
7. Serve with ice cream or with whipped cream after cooling for 15 minutes.

51 - Old Fashioned Rhubarb Dump Cake

Rhubarb gives this cake a heartiness and texture that is simply divine. Try it served with whipped cream to complement the fullness of the cake.

Ingredients:

- 1/3 cup (80 ml) butter or margarine, melted
- 3 oz (84 g) strawberry flavored gelatin
- ½ cup (120 ml) sugar
- 1 cup (240 ml) water
- 1 lb (450 g) fresh rhubarb, chopped
- 18.25 oz (500 g) white cake mix

Directions:

1. Turn the oven to 350°F (180°C).
2. Pull out a 9x13 inch (22.5x32.5 cm) glass or metal baking dish.

3. Place the rhubarb in the bottom of the dish, spreading evenly.
4. Sprinkle with gelatin and sugar.
5. Mix together the cake mix, water and butter with a whisk. Blend well.
6. Pour the mix over the rhubarb, spreading evenly and covering rhubarb completely, but not mixing.
7. Bake for 45 minutes, or slightly longer if using a glass dish, until the top is golden brown.
8. Serve warm, topped with whipped cream.

Thank You

If you enjoyed the recipes, please consider leaving a review of the book. Good reviews encourage an author to write as well as help books to sell. Good reviews can be just a few short sentences describing what you liked about the book. If you could spend 30 seconds writing a review, I would appreciate it. You can review this title right now at your favorite retailer.

Other Books by Brianne Heaton

- 56 Breakfast Sandwich Recipes: Irresistible Sandwich Ideas to Kickstart Your Morning

- 50 Holiday Dessert Recipes: Delectable Dessert Ideas For The Christmas Holidays And Other Special Occasions

- 51 Easter Dessert Ideas: Scrumptious Easter Recipes For Any Occasion

- 46 Sriracha Flavored Recipes: Delicious Sriracha Hot Sauce Cookbook For A Spicy Palate

Get the latest update on new releases from the author at:

https://www.brianneheaton.com/newsletter

About the Author – Brianne Heaton

Brianne Heaton started off collecting recipes that her family and friends enjoyed. After receiving many requests for copies of the recipes, she decided to share them by writing recipes books that everyone would appreciate.

Visit Brianne's website at:

https://www.brianneheaton.com/

Connect with Brianne Heaton

I really appreciate you reading my book! Here are my social media contact information:

Friend me on Facebook: https://www.facebook.com/BrianneHeatonRecipeBooks/

Follow me on Twitter: https://twitter.com/brianneheaton

Check me out on Goodreads: https://www.goodreads.com/author/show/8121938.Brianne_Heaton

Subscribe to my newsletter: https://www.brianneheaton.com/newsletter/

Visit my website: https://www.brianneheaton.com/

www.ingramcontent.com/pod-product-compliance
Lightning Source LLC
Chambersburg PA
CBHW062103290426
44110CB00022B/2695